Star-Eyed Fool

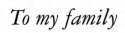

To my family

Star-Eyed Fool

Hill farming on Exmoor and Dartmoor
1939–2004

Jane Beeson

Millennium Awards

THE MINT PRESS

TARKA·COUNTRY
MILLENNIUM AWARDS

First published in Great Britain by The Mint Press, 2004

ISBN 1-903356-37-7

Cataloguing in Publication Data
CIP record for this title is available from the British Library

The Mint Press
18 The Mint
Exeter, Devon
England EX4 3BL

Cover design by Delphine Jones

Main cover illustration: Ford Farm, Dartmoor
Text design and typesetting by Topics–The Creative Partnership, Exeter
Printed and bound in Great Britain by Short Run Press Ltd, Exeter

CONTENTS

INTRODUCTION

I t was suggested to me I write a book of interest to the local area and visitors by the Tarka Country Millennium Award representative (the Tarka Country Millennium Awards are led by the Tarka Country Trust and are mainly funded by lottery money through the Millennium Commission). At first I had only in mind a poetry collection but felt this had been covered by *Moor Poets*, Pat Fleming's excellent collection of local poets.

Then I had an idea that might be of general interest to people living in and visiting the West – I could compare my life as a child on a hill farm on Exmoor during the Second World War years to my life as an adult on a hill farm on Dartmoor. A daunting prospect but I thought that it was unique enough to be of interest, and that the emphasis would be on poetry using prose as a link.

Acknowledgements are due to **Headland**, also to poetry magazines that have used my work in the past – and most recently to *Moor Poets*, supported by a Tarka Country Millennium Award in 2003. I should like to thank Colin and Hazel Pearse for their hill-farming knowledge and information; Mark Beeson for his time spent in the selection of my poetry; and Peter Beeson for his patience with my computer skills. Also, Dr Tom Greeves and John Weir for their advice, help and letters in support of my project. Others who kindly wrote letters of support were Professor Peter Thomson, Elizabeth Hurst and poets Roselle Angwin and Pat Fleming.

Lastly, my 'little' brother, Euan Bowater, for helping me with memories.

I should like to thank Tarka Country Millennium Awards for funding, and the organisers for their help and encouragement for this book.

JANE BEESON

Exmoor
1939–45

In the half-light

In the clouded days of memory
in the growing light of morning
I lay on my bed looking at a pine tree's branches
changing shape in the wind
its spurs stabbed like fighting cocks
to scratch a jig-saw out of white sky.

My pillow humped in hills, my damp hair
stuck to my face: the ruckles in my sheet
felt like caterpillars crawling
and I knew I was neither asleep nor awake
but in the half-light of day-dream
where the rustle of pine-needles brushing slates
was the tramp of animals in the long grass
and boulders crouched like people.

Sunlight whorled through leaded windows
blinding my eyes, dazzling my senses.
I lowered child's legs on a cold floor
pulled back my nest of bedclothes
climbed on the sill to see
a spruce tree straight as a drilling soldier
its branches stilled to the drum

of my father's feet on the polished stair
calling me out of my underworld.

WAR

*I stood in the pantry against the sink, my mother stood
beside the ironing board.*

*'It's war,' she said, 'war's declared. The Germans
have marched into Poland.'*

*I listened, felt their dread, experienced my own
excitement – evacuation to the country. Exmoor – perhaps
a pony.*

I was nine.

*Heather, honey-bees, sun, clouds racing – my
imagination soared to join the skylarks. Reality came
later – rain, snow, darkness, a cold house lit by oil
lamps, long days of loneliness, of reading, of hunger, of
fear. Primarily fear.*

*Once established in a farmhouse on the brink of
Exmoor – some called it 'the heart' – my mother, devoid
of my father, moved with her portable wireless as some
take a lapdog. It followed her from room to room always
talking, bringing news of the war; its voice was the voice
I heard most often.*

*My father moved his paper-making office from London
to Surrey, became an air-raid warden, rang my mother*

once a week on Sunday, told of high explosives down the garden, windows blown in, incendiaries in the loft he gathered before they exploded. Of sirens and nights huddled in the 'dug out' – the fall-out of the Blitz.

By 1940 my mother, a Suffolk farmer's daughter, had combined the 40 acres that came with the farmhouse with the local farming neighbour's land and was working it in conjunction with him. He, in turn, was glad of extra land. The country was crying out for home grown food. Farming had been ignored owing to foreign imports since the First World War and now was suddenly faced by the probability of starvation. Convoys bringing supplies from America and Canada were being sunk in the Atlantic, the government was eager to pay our farmers to make the country self-sufficient – grow food.

The result: a flurry of farming activity. The old shire horses were worked as never before, rusting machinery they had once pulled was oiled and put back into action. Tractors as yet were few in hill farming areas, they were too expensive for the average hill farmer without government support, and not particularly suitable for steep small fields; in spite of this the Case, the David Brown and the Fordson began to be seen. The next to come was the Ferguson some years later, that became known as the 'Fergie'.

*I had a pony to ride and Exmoor to explore – a realised
dream with a sting in its tail, for it didn't come without
isolation and loneliness. My brother, barely four, was
hardly a companion and occupied our nanny's time –
Nanny, who had been our mother's nanny, and was to live
with us till she died.*

*I didn't go to school those first War years so it was
loneliness that drove me to read, to day-dream, to seek
and adapt myself to almost any friend that came my
way: local children, other evacuees, adults who called on
my mother, all alleviated my isolated world...*

Mrs Crocker banged on
the door with her umbrella
'Conna? Are you in?'
My mother slid into the kitchen,
my father slunk in the woodshed.
'Won't you come in, Mrs Crocker' I asked.
Serpent-like she advanced over the floor
'Shall I sit down?'
'Yes, please sit down.'
'I'll get you out a sweet' –
she held a melting sweet
offered on her palm.

I sat and talked to Mrs Crocker
who banged on the floor
with her umbrella
until my mother came
and poured the tea.
'Conna' she said, 'It's so good
of you, Conna.'

A fox-fur wound
Mrs Crocker's neck
as she walked down the cobbles
waving her umbrella.

*I envied the other children, some local some evacuated, who
went to the village school and hung on the rails of the
village green in gangs. With difficulty and by devious means
I contrived to join them – but it took time. And when you're
young time passes slowly. So I was not only involved in
talking to people my mother didn't want to, but inevitably
became absorbed into hill farming. Any diversion that
required leaving the farm was an excitement, entertainment
other than animals and pony riding was unknown – we
made our own games out of imagination and anything to
hand. So for me going to farm sales, auctions, the markets,
the yearly Exmoor pony sales at Bampton, was a treat.*

The Sale

'3 I'm bid, 3, 3, 3
Five is it? Thank you, sir
5, 5, 5 pounds I'm bid for the chestnut sucker.
Six on my left. 6, 6, 6
seven, seven, seven – eight on your right
8, 8, 8 – 9 is it. Nine, nine '

The bidding rose, the voice sang out
faces round the ring froze in concentration –
a blink, a half nod, a lifted eye-lid
the auctioneer's repetition grew longer and faster
his hammer lifted, smacked down

'Chestnut sucker. Mr Bowden'
His helper noted it down.

The 'gate' opened, the terrified pony skidded on straw
        fell, recovered, scampered from the ring through a
                                                lane of rails

The crowd relaxed – another pony entered the ring
more spectators crowded in behind the bidders.
'Young horse pony, 4 years last May. Twenty pound,
who'll give me twenty?'

Cloth-capped farmers in jackets and polished gaiters
leant forward on the rail.

Then an Arab mare led by a groom
arched its perfect neck like a Dorset fossil,
stamped a delicate limb. Its silk mane drifted
on air, nostrils quivered in a hint of a neigh.
The auctioneer settled his palms on his box
smiled his satisfaction, looked round at the crowd
as if before him stood Cleopatra

'There you are, ladies and gents, you can see for
                                        yourselves
there never was a prettier Arab filly. Five hundred
                                        pounds?'

'Cheap at the price, gentlemen. Come on then,
                        what'll you bid me?'

'A hundred, one hundred I'm bid. One hundred,
                        100, 100...'

*My mother was happy farming, it became her 'war
effort'. She loved animals and had absorbed knowledge
from growing up on her father's farm, but knew little*

about the climate that went with hill farming. About that
we were all to learn...

Hedging

My mother held a bill hook like a man
knew her way around the hedges, chose her stem
laid it uphill to fill a gap

her dress was always the same, belted overalls, boots –
hair netted, rigid as stone
in its simplicity

My job, to pull away the trimmings
drag them unwilling to a patch decided
pile them awkward and whipping back
into a heap for burning

the heap grew – I tired of it

Intent up in the hedge
my mother split and bent
the smaller limbs
weaving layers

I knelt on the ground, ripped the match across

                                  the rough

lit paper and straw. A flame. Smoke rose
in a pungent curl, the ash sticks caught

Up the hedge, one hand round a limb,

                                 my mother's wave

indicated the littered ground beneath

The wind changed. I ran chased by smoke.

*I was ten. My own war effort started with leading the
carthorse. We consisted of a team of eight, two on top of
the wagon, two others pitching hay up on either side,
myself temporarily in charge of the massive horse – or it
seemed so to me...*

The carthorse surged its white-foamed chest
lunged into the traces like a wave
that slowly mounts its crest and thrusts
towards the shore. And I, reaching
to the bridle leapt forward with it
fearful that my feet might crunch beneath iron

Sweat-wetted hair sleeked my face
like a cork I bobbed

engulfed by flies and sun, carried ahead
of the oncoming wheel. 'Whoa'
the shout came as the boom of sea in a cave –
juddering, the horse halted and I with it
my body strained as wire

Rivulets of salt trickled into my mouth
a wall of hay rose behind me.

*A smallholding named Liddycleave perched drunkenly on
the steep lane beneath Yealscombe, our leased farmhouse,
and it was in conjunction with the owners, Alec and
Eadie, that we farmed. Alec, as a farmer, was exempted
from call-up; he kept a small flock of sheep and five
milking cows. With our land, and some added young
cattle, it was enough to manage because all the young men
who worked on the farms were called up; the once
numerous helpers in the hayfields no longer existed, the
work was done by the old and the very young – and it
was hard because the land was dependent on a labour
force for its profitable running, whether in the hayfields
or sowing and weeding roots.*

*Gradually Land Girls from the Land Army arrived
in desultory ones and twos, but the men weren't used to
working with women and didn't like to ask them to do*

heavy work. I do remember my mother though, walking
backwards and forwards across a field sowing with a
fiddle (an action with a bow similar to playing a violin
but used to broadcast seeds) – I presume we had no horse
drill. Scythes were used to cut the smaller fields and open
up round the gateways for the horse-drawn mower or
reaper so not to cause any waste.

Milking

The milking cows stood in straw
dung splattered the concrete gully

A woman sat on a stool her head pressed against a
                                                    flank
her fingers created the inimitable sound
of milk on milk in a bucket

She nodded at me as I stood in the doorway
her long neck stretched away from the cow to see me
the backs of her hands were freckled, her fingers
                                                    cracked

Two Jerseys, one Guernsey, a single Friesian
made up the herd of their holding

that clasped the side of a cleave like an awkward
brooch –
one side their roof met the rising hill
the other a chimney rose up to sky –
it was definitely lopsided

A child
I gazed and gazed –
it worried me. I tried to straighten it, make it a house
in a house's shape. Outside was a small concrete yard
with a ringer and a drain
to tip away the washing water
that flowed down the lane
too steep to stand on –
in autumn a water-shoot
in winter an ice sheet
trapping the cows in their building till spring.

Above the farm a tall feathery ash quivered.

Fifty foot beneath on the valley floor the Exe
snaked slowly, ate away sandy banks
formed impenetrable pools under craning trees
raised shingle islands.

*Yealscombe was long and low, supposedly made up of two
cottages joined together with a central porch. In front a
cobbled yard sloped up to the oddly added bow-window
projecting on to the cobbles from the main room. The
eastern side of the porch had an upstairs, the west reduced
itself to a ground floor only. It was thatched and covered
in ivy. Inside, the two ends of the interior were joined by a
long dark passage lit by a single oil lamp – the bathroom
was half way along. It was a scaring walk for a child
needing to visit it at night, and I would brave it clutching
my candle, hoping the flame wouldn't be blown out by the
draft that always blew. My room was a cold little white
room like a cell with upright bars on the window's opening
light. But I could hear the trickle of the water trough
outside which I loved.*

*When I wasn't outside, my domain was mostly the
buildings containing a room beyond the stables and stalls
that I had to screw my courage to enter...*

The harness room

was hung with stags' heads
dust and cobwebs draped their antlers like dirty lace –
rat holes leered from the skirting-boards.

The rabbit hutches stood in a stall
a bran bin stood against the wall.

At nights I went alone to feed the rabbits
gave hay to the pony, listened to the snort
and stamp of the carthorses
focused the torch beam through
the harness room door –

king rats sat
tapered tails stretched
their small eyes glittered

In the bran bin a mouse had a nest
of micelings naked, pink and wriggling
I picked one up, examined long legs
miniature claws, a stub of a tail
its sealed eyes bulged like a bluebottle's

By torchlight
the buildings seemed a house of vermin

It was better in the summer with the bats
in jerky flight with a squeak the pitch
of a rusting hinge – evenings were hot
and the air enclosed like ermine

The clamouring rabbits fed
I left relieved to breathe the sky of stars

Cassiopeia, the Pleiades, the Plough
shone in the blue-black night
Orion's dagger flashed its jewels –
enthralled, with neck bent back
I zig-zagged over the moon-smoothed cobbles
under the mazy white of the Milky Way.

*I didn't like the darkness of buildings, nor of woods with
tall trunks and shadows. I liked to be in the open,
whether it was day or night. I was also acutely aware of
scents and smells as a child – they played an important
part in my life and though I liked sheep I hated their
smell. Now I'm hardly aware of it.*

*The sheep sales generally took place in a nearby village,
for there was no transport except by foot or in a horse drawn
cart netted over to secure sheep or pigs. The cattle were
walked but generally went to more formal markets with
proper pens and an auctioneers' box, though on occasion they
were sold in a market street simply ringed by people.*

Walking sheep to the Sales

I remember the sickening reek
of thirty sheep, black droppings dotting the road.
Following, I held my breath, tried not to inhale
                         urine's wet-sweet smell

The hedge branches met over us
made a dark tunnel – a stop, a block
the startled sheep turned – surged
                         a horse-and-cart filled the lane

Pressed into the hedge
I felt my lack of size, regretted the stick
knocked from my hand –
                         the driver's unrelenting face

A dulled hiss of air, a deadened thud
of slotted feet as the sheep pounded back
with frightened half-wooled over eyes –
                         their smell enveloped

In a gateway where hurdles divided the field
where sheep were urged in pens and farmers
plunged their hands in wool, prodded, lifted
                    struggling 'two-tooths' to other folds –

a boy with a back-to-front cap forced back
a sheep's lip – I saw two white teeth
with yellow-pink gums in the centre –

                    the sheep was panting

the boy had taken his cap off and was scratching

On Exmoor it was seldom dry for long, and one autumn
I remember it raining non-stop for six weeks. One of the
mysteries to me, and apparently to my mother, was a gipsy
caravan by the river on the land opposite ours. As a child
I couldn't imagine anything I desired more than to live
in it...

Under alder in a meadow
in an arm's curve of river
stood a gipsy caravan. Built of wood
with black roof arching, shafts waiting
painted yellow
with window, door and platform beckoning
a perfect plaything for a child –
I dreamt of nights beside the river.

I ran through the thistle fields
above the steep ridged cleave

to gaze down on the caravan
as if a jewel on the snake's head

One night I dreamt it taken
swallowed by the river, dragged
bit by bit, jerked apart like doll's limbs,
carried through banks of fishermen,
eased with a rush between
bridge buttresses to float
in painted planks out to sea.

In flood ...

a roar announced the river –
peat water hunched its centre
spliced like rope: chocolate wave
sucked wave curled like cocks' combs

The clapper lay gapped,
two massive slabs deflected
one down stream, the other upended –
a mattress jerked from its bed

Snow clung in patches
on the hill's face. A boy,

fingers hooked in a pony's mane,
braved its pitted floor.

A day later sun struck mica.
The river split on an
island's prow, chassied
down a tunnel of trees.

*When Coleridge wrote 'Spring comes slowly up this way' he
could have been writing about Exmoor. Certainly summer
was wayward – as soon as you thought it had come it had
gone leaving gloom and despondency in its wake. 'No
summer' everyone grumbled – then suddenly it was there
again...*

Fields ...

each field had a name, Well Park, Long Down,
Cleaver Piece, Homer Meadow, Stone Slade Plat –
each field was a different size, a different shape

Docks grew tall, tight grazed between –
where sheep had been
the land had a different look
a different smell where they clustered for shade

along the banks
or for a drift of air against gates, panting –
Closewools and Exmoor Horns

Early the grass fields showed grey
later the sun greened them

Beech grew on the banks, cut back thick on the sides
thinned to trees in the centre like a man's hair
Gateways varied
dry and stony or water-filled ruts –
with sandalled feet I climbed around the posts

The cleave descended
falling in ridges to the river
wildflowers grew on ground like dried-up cloth
butterflies vied for them –
nettles and rusting machinery disputed field corners,
picked-up horse shoes hung on gates
dropping out luck

It used to worry me, all that wasted luck

Cows lay with stomachs bulged methodically chewing
small calves lay out flat, deaf till I got up close

then leapt like deer, galloped, turned to face me –
when I walked between the cows they never shifted
only turned a head, twitched an ear
eyes blackened by flies

I smelt their sour-sweet steamy breath
and contentment.

*I can't remember much about the autumn but I'll never
forget that first icy winter in a house lit by oil lamps,
heated by primitive oil stoves carried from room to room
(always giving off oil fumes I hated), and one wood or
peat fire in the evenings in the sitting-room. The fireplace
in the dining room where we ate, although being
thoughtfully screened from the draft that came down the
stairs, could never be lit because it smoked – not a little
but in thick grey clouds.*

Snow 1940

I woke to silence. Light.
Walls whiter, the white ceiling tinged by green –
windows snow lined
snow driven in on the sill unthawed

Under blankets I absorbed the change –

wondered
Out of bed, out of the window
I gazed on the undulating white blanket
the still-running trough. No walls.

A dark row of firs held up laden branches
like frosted chocolate

*

'The quiet' they said, the local people
when the snow came. Certainly
the ducks were quiet, the chickens
and the sparrows. The light
was white as white
and snow threaded its way
through branches, alighting
on some. Sun glowed
in a yellow haze, faded
to whiteness: flakes came again
thicker and faster.

Stark and grey
unhappiness rules the day:
there is a darkness that ends
in a night of the soul –
there is play that ends in dream.

The banks' shadow is black –
a hard line of sun marks its edge –
as a child I played
the too-short days away,
see-sawed on a log laid over a hedge
with a new-found friend.

The wonder of night
when we talked in the dark
the lack of need for sleep
the dew-moist grass of early morning
the pattern of footsteps
leading through a gateway to ever more fields
that stretch into an expanding distance –
the din of nature
resounding in a child's ears
breeding a dread of repression
of the aridity of the classroom
of knowledge taught, not lived.

Craving snow in the nights of winter,
sliding from rucked sheets
to the cold floors of morning –
breathing on the panes
to melt the ornate decor
of frost on glass, designs of fern
and forest delicate as lace.

To dress shivering in an iced room
hasten down to kitchen's warmth –
feet pushed in boots, hands mitted
the great door pulled open
to draw in winter's breath
revel in nature's changed face
printed with blue shadow –
search out the deepest snow,
plunge up to knees, to thighs,
forming snowballs that fall apart
the snow too cold to gel.

To lick the crust on top of walls,
follow hare-tracks loping in the lea
of the bank, stamping beside them
marking in ecstasy
the isolated silent landscape
of winter.

The sun's rising glitter
reflecting on ice, colouring
shade mauve, the sky bluing –
the single stark tree on the bank
thawed in sun's strength –
the twitter of wrens shifting
along hedgerows, searching
for warmth. Sheep bleat
on the hill trailing yellow against
snow's whiteness: yellow ducks flounder
slithering to black-holed water
in the pond's centre.

The house window opens.
A voice calls. Reluctantly
leaving the brave new world of winter
for house's enveloping warmth
I ease scarlet toes
out of wet socks, lay my hands
on the stove as if a mother
offering comfort, its living gurgle
increased by an east wind.

Ivy pushes feelers under the eaves –
a fire dwindles from wet wood
sinks on a mound of ash.
The vitality of childhood batters
on a window with long closed shutters

Snow thawed ...
the lane turned to rivulets of water, sliding,
                              dividing and reuniting
slithering under gates, forming sand tongues,
                                   spilling over

Oak-leaves opened late
black ash buds later. I used to think the big ash dead
standing alone in a field like a Rembrandt etching

until one night with the moon rising
it showed feathery leaves like dancers' fingers
almost as if it liked the moon's light on a dark
                                        backcloth

Cows came out of their winter stalls
caked-dung lined their hocks, dangled from bellies –
I longed to clean them

Fields of grass did it
or scissors and a hard bristle brush –
the cows winced and cow-kicked
Eadie slapped them, shouted.
With her hand she turned the scalded
skimmed-off cream to butter –
rolled it oozing blue-white milk
patted it with ridged boards
into barrel coils

*

Down the steep cleave the grass colour changes
slim ditches cross the side in ruled lines
spaced wide

Ditches bleed, runnels open over dried grass
water trickles through mud banks
creates emerald

Ewes surge through the gate
push past, hasten on to lush grass, tear it absorbed
followed by the insistent high pitched call of lambs

Moving among them I hear the rapid munch
feel their distracted anxious shifting on.
Bleats cease. Lamb-tails contort with sucking

*

March born lambs played the water meadows
leaping, legs braced
raced in a crazy follow-my-leader game up a hedge

Alec (Eadie's man) stormed out with a piece of
blackthorn
blocked the hole

swore

pushed the ewes up on top
where the wind caught them –
bleats drowned speech, Jessie barked

We stayed on the cold down
till their cries ceased except for a whine of wind
the rustle of dead leaves under banks

'Won't they be cold?' I asked
Alec stood in the gateway counting –
finished, counted again, looked at me

In bed I cried for the lambs
certain the cold would get them

A day later sun joined the east wind
made the ground dry as a treat – said Alec.

Then suddenly life changed. My mother had found me a school...

like a dark cloud that looms
comes nearer and suddenly is overhead with no gap
                                                    of sky –
A weekly boarder. Minehead. A convent.
Nuns in black robes, chains clanking, crosses
                                                    dangling
dark mornings in chapel, cold, hunger
At nights I dreamt of chocolate
the lessons I couldn't do
I'd missed two years of school.

I was to catch a bus in on Monday and one out on
Friday. My mother was to meet me in the village –
Exford – our village as we thought of it. All the children
were Roman Catholics. They didn't take to me though
I doubt it was because I wasn't Catholic – I was
probably just alien and odd. Sister Celina was kind,
beautiful and young and used to brush my hair at nights.
I was horrified when she told me all hers had been
shaved off.

Fortunately my time there ended after two terms. I
couldn't swallow at nights, so even my mother, who was no

great psychologist, realised there was something wrong as I
was perfectly able to swallow during my weekends home.
    At home joy – my own sort of joy – resumed...

Early in the year the moor smelt of peat
gave me a sharp quickening, a catch of breath
as I rode above Pitsworthy, through Wellshead fields
followed the Dunkery road to Alderman's Barrow.

The heather rose waist high
with stems like rusting springs
laid out like a carpet-runner stretching
to the beacon and Codsend enclosure
wavy with white bog grass and a gate
with a track where we cantered our ponies,
Susan and I – my new-found friend who came
to the village, stayed, rode a black pony
bare-back, unbridled –
up and down the valley we rode
at the back of the Crown hotel
our fingers wound in the pony's mane,
both together, Susan and I, till she went back
to school – and our shared life died.

My mother now learned of a new evacuated Jewish school
in the village. I pleaded to be allowed to go to the village

school but my mother was adamant – she didn't like all
those 'rough' boys which really was indicative of the
pervasive class difference of those times that made such a
school unacceptable to her. It is also true that the
sanitation of most moorland schools up until the '60s was
excessively primitive and had to be seen to be believed.

So the evacuated school it was. But at home our father
was down on a rare visit and the conversation about the
farm vied with the War for importance.

The Grey Carthorses

'He's scared' my mother said, 'scared of the horses
he admitted to me he couldn't work them.'

My father picked a tooth. 'We could get a tractor.'

'A tractor?' My mother, wedded to horses
expressed her shock, 'A tractor will never work
                                        these fields –
they're much too steep.'

A month later a Fordson tractor stood in the yard.
My mother sized it up. 'It won't go through the
                                        gates, it's too wide.'

The two greys still in the stables, flighty and tall,
stamped
and twitched, jerked hay from their racks, snorted
blew spray from their nostrils.

'When are the greys going?' my father asked
'Next week. To Dulverton.' My mother's voice was
tragic.

'It's the end for horses' she prophesied.
And so it was.

*From where or how we acquired that tractor I don't know.
There were not many around; it may even have been
shipped over from America. But the sad story was that its
end came by fire. It lived at the top of Yealscombe lane in a
shed that had been built as a garage by the house's owners,
the lane down to the house being considered too steep to
descend before car brakes were more trustworthy. One night
the tractor caught fire and both it and the shed burnt – in
the morning all that was left was a black skeleton tractor.
The Fire engine didn't arrive quickly, if at all, and a
tractor must have been difficult to replace in the War.*

*It was summer when I went to my new school in the
village. Using the lanes was no problem for children*

*except for the local gang of young boys. There was only
the occasional van and few cars. I had never heard of
threatening men, in fact it would be true to say that
unless one existed within a family, they simply weren't
heard of by country children. With no television we lived
in innocence. The walk to the school in the village was
about a mile and a half, perhaps a little more. I went by
bicycle or pony; sometimes I just walked. Later on I took
my little brother with me. Altogether I must have stayed
at that unusual school, to which I shall always be
indebted, for about 3½ years before being finally banished
to a boarding school.*

The Walk to School

Yellow-hammers shifted
beside me along the hedges,
their high shrill song
permeated air: I splayed
branches to discover the singers
who ceased always before
the last syllable. Kicked stones
bounced over the grassed centre
clattered to rest in front of cow-dung,
host to a buzz of flies

At the corner, the lane slipped
sideways, gauged channels crossed
bald rock where water flowed

Pig-squeals sounded
from breeze-block buildings –
wind waved the tall ash
as I ran under, thudding down
the lane beside a stream
running in a gully
to the ford

Wagtails balanced on boulders
tails bouncing like toys –
in the peat dark river
trout idled at the pool's head
drifted back under hazel
where gnats danced in darkness
rising up and up only to fall
like Sisiphus
to mount again

Barefoot in ice water
dazzled by pebbles' shine
I scooped them in my hands –

sun-dulled they slid through
my fingers like happiness
or a fading dream

Extracting numbed feet
I tied shoelaces against the mile's
walk to school

The Stone Throwers

I gazed, a child at the window
leaning out, looking on the trough,
listening to the water's trickle
where bubbles rose, dissolved
to rise again in the clear dark tank

I dipped my hands, splashed my eyes,
my face, clearing away sleep
for the morning that shone
on worn cobbles sloped down
to a line of firs in front
of the water-meadow: slim ditches
crossed the hill, spilled over
staining the grass emerald
like splashes on a pale green dress

Balanced on tufts over poached ground
leading to a lane spattered in cow-dung,
I reached the ford where
trout lounged
drifting back on the current,
tails propelling them forward
under a scum of foam

Satchel swinging, dragging leaden
feet, I left the looping river
for blue-black tarmac
avoiding islands of horse-droppings

Foxgloves craned freckled horns
seducing bumble bees: tugging out
white-stemmed grass, I sucked idly
to a yellow hammer's wheeze

In a shadow of arched-over hedges
a barrier of boys blocked the way
chanting threats, chucking stones –
feet and heartbeats mingled
thudding past the house in nettles,
shadows stretched like clawing brambles

Terraced houses rose to comfort –
a girl's dress lifted on her thighs
as her rhythmic legs drove
the swing on the Green

From school we regularly went out along the lanes
gathering foxglove leaves because they were considered of
value for use as medication for wounded soldiers...

The Foxgloves ...

climbed the banks in forests
and we, with our sacks dragging,
gathered leaves, stuffed them
full to bursting, pulled string
round their necks, left
stripped stems displaying
bells speckled maroon

There was something sad
about the bank
after we had demolished it –
after we had torn away
the leaves, left the flowers
like poor bare girls
with artful faces

In July came shearing followed by dipping about a month
later. It happened approximately at the same time every
year according to weather; also the availability of the dip
which was shared by most of the small farmers around,
including Alec.

At the time the dip powder was based on arsenic and
consequently my mother was nervous of allowing us near
it, so my view was birds-eye from the cleave above. The
dip was set alongside the Exe in a flat area between the
road and river next Silly Bridge and approached by
Muddicombe Lane (as children we always hurried past
ruined Muddicombe because rumour had it a young girl
had drowned herself in the well, for lost love, no doubt.
Certainly since then it appeared to have been let go to a
ruin). Silly Bridge was small, humped, and incredibly
narrow, and was the pivot of a Z bend, the road folding
back sharply on either side. The dip was filled by river
water and when the dipping was finally complete, the
reddened water was let back into the Exe in a slow thin
trickle. Days later the trickle still continued it being
thought at the time, less likely to poison the fish...

Shearing

The back of the barn was full of shadow
where fleeces mounted sensual as piled cloud.

A figure bent over a white-faced sheep
steered his long-knifed clippers through its coat,
opened it, folded it back –
his hand moved across the belly
exposing the white of the wool, the pale pink
flesh like a peeled fruit.

Bit by bit the fleece fell away
no nicks, no cuts, no pause till it dropped
in one piece, a coat that had wrapped
a sheep for a year. The shearer uncurled,
straightened, a hand on his back
waited for the next – the sheep uncovered
walked to a corner, stood bewildered
head hung down with thin white legs –
its great-coat flung on a board for rolling.

Another was seized – a thud of feet as they
                                        scattered
each caught in turn, dragged to the shearer
who wiped sweat-matted hair from a weather
                                        dried face.

Grey stoned walls framed a woman kneeling
on sacking bags stitched in a carpet,

turning in and rolling each fleece like an art
tying each one with wool pulled, rough spun.

Dipping ...

panting sheep penned tightly
frightened eyes, the smell of dip –
grabbed, dragged
each sheep caught by its horns,
lifted, dropped in the dip.
A splash, the swimming sheep
immersed, pushed under by a crutch,
turned, steered swimming
to struggle out up steps, stand dripping
shaking the dip from their fleece
in pink-red mist

The dip empties, bleeds
a slow thin trickle into the river

Brown trout lie in the dark of ignorance
in a network of hidden roots and pools.

Hay followed. I don't know that it was the idyll people remember because it was always fraught with the fear of rain, and wet hay in a rick went mouldy or burnt. There was no baler so the hay was still thrown up by pitchforks and a rick built. If it was late, harvest seemed to follow close on its tail...

Oats grew in shining fields
heads jostled, swayed, rustled in wind –
in storm it swirled, flattened,
left raw gapped patches.
When the cutter came
bell heads dropped crestfallen
till knotted with twisted straw
they lay in sheaves like a neck
drawn tight by a scarf

Out of the fields came rabbits
mice, lapwing and curlew – and rats
running from the pale spiked stubble
to be shot with smoking guns

We built the shivering corn in stooks of four
worked noiseless except for the sheaves rustle
heads tangled like beaded hair – worked on

into the velvet night till the harvest moon
rose in a huge white ball and we let drop
our scratched hands to look it full in the face

*September – and a day of excitement and flurry when the
threshing machine appeared, both expected and
unexpected, depending always on how much had got done
at a farm elsewhere the day before. In the past threshing
had been done in a round house with horses or a donkey
walking round and round – or simply by beating either
on a winnowing plank floor across a barn between two
doors (as we have at Easdon) to provide a draft; or even
through the drafty central passage of a longhouse. But in
the 1940s, a traction engine arrived in the lane behind
the barn to drive the belt of the thresher set up inside.
With it came five workers...*

In the central barn
in the twin-winged yard
we waited.

Up in the lane
the traction engine
blew and snuffled, shunted steam

Down beneath
came the murmur of talk.
Then like a dead thing jerking a muscle
the threshing machine lived –
the belt pulled, grew faster and faster
the barn came alive
everything shook

Against midnight rafters
dust and husks floated in darkness –
corn poured down a shoot to the bin.
Someone grabbed me, pulled

'Do 'ee want'er itch, scratch like a bitch?
T'will drive 'ee mazed – they husks'

I looked regretfully at the shoot
corn hissing, rattling, falling
sacks hooked on, dragged away, tied
shifted like bodies to the back of the barn
The talk – a fear of rats biting sacking –
gold corn pouring like gold coins falling
And still dust dancing, rising, drifting
– the scratching, the itching

The belt hurt my ears. The big door slammed
on oat nuggets rising in bulged out sacks –
the dominant machine cut off at the last
with a dying death-rattle

Workers washed
dirt-caked arms, necks, and faces
caught and lost the amber soap
sliding through their fingers leaving
smoke-blue bubbles clouding
a tank of water running

drank tea or cider, lounged –
or knees bound by arms
sat contented
laughed, smoked –

threshing over till noon tomorrow

*In the War deer hunting was reduced (I notice it is always
called 'stag' hunting but in fact in autumn it was the
custom to hunt hinds. Presumably it is better for its image
not to let the public be informed of this) – the deer it was
agreed, were to be kept in check by being shot by farmers if*

necessary. They did endless damage to farmers' crops and could jump almost any height of fence. As a child I used to go out with the 'tufters' (a small bunch of experienced hounds) on a pony, which was interesting for learning about deers' habitat and behaviour; only a few farmers and local people went with them. Their purpose was generally to pick out the chosen stag for culling already traced, in the early hours of the morning or night before, by the 'harbourer'. I have to say while I perfectly understand the importance of careful deer control, I saw enough of hunting, particularly hind hunting, to find it impossible to see as a sport. Aged eleven on a pony, I was the only person present when a hind stood trapped in the thick undergrowth of Culbone woods, hounds baying and leaping at her with no master, huntsman or hunt official present to call hounds off or shoot her. The effect on me was lasting and I have never had anything to do with a hunt since.

Local people shook their heads, surmised a hard winter. And certainly winters of the forties were some of the hardest winters in living memory...

The weather cock...

turned south-east

Sky thickened, turned a dead grey
it was quiet as quiet, no birds shifted –
the tall firs next the buildings stiffened

A blizzard came in the night.
In the morning snow closed the windows
the front door was sealed by driven snow.

We dug a path from back to front with spades and
                                                  a grubber –
an old man came to help, his legs bound with canvas
a sack on his bent-over back, his cap turned round

We children floundered puppy-happy in drifts
hammered in vain the water-trough's thickened ice –
the pipe in the bank had stopped running –
the cold pipe in the house was frozen –
only the well in the pantry remained
we pumped it, waited for sun.

Out of the quiet came flakes – one, then two,
                                         then more
until the whole sky filled. Our tongues stuck out
we caught the flakes, others clung on our clothes
painted us white except for our crimson faces

I neither felt nor remembered the cold
until indoors the lighted fire
thawed my toes and fingers
filled my eyes with tears of unforgotten pain.

Days turned to weeks and still the snow trapped us.

Snow...

                              came again in February
a world of white silencing the small cold birds
that flocked to the yard for pickings
silently, quietly, new snow wrapped us –

Under the line of firs it thinned
so the ground showed black
and boughs dusted gates
that held a crust like sugar icing

Drifts rose where the wind had driven
climbing a gate I sank to my waist
in a drift with a blown curve
shaped like a knife

Telegraph poles snapped or leant
broken branches lined the ditches –

cut off from communication
we walked a world of isolation

Farmers with reddened skins
in unshaved faces
dug out sheep along the hedges –
cattle in the buildings breathed steam,
or in the yard urinated
merging virgin white
to pools of slush with yellow edges

The thaw came
and the lane ran like a water-slide –
booted and scarved we walked
the once white road spoiled with slush
wheels showed tarmac in shining ribbons
drooping grass lined the banks, trees dripped

*

With electric lines down, the school-room chilled –
huddled round the table, knees drawn up, socked
                                       feet frozen
we cherished the fitful green-wood fire that spat in
                                       the grate

clutched our hands round mugs of watery coco,
                                        cried for the pain
in our thawing fingers, wiped our running noses
sat rocking, each in our icy coracle longing for
                                        the bell
that freed us, sent us home

The boarders, children of Jewish descent
evacuated with the school from Kent
had parents 'detained in Germany'
awaited their release when the war was over
unaware of the holocaust, their parents' fate
for no one told them because no one knew
                                not in nineteen forty two
Yet even as a child I sensed some evil hidden
half-guessed what Eva and Renata never said.

*Summer came at last. It changed us all. Summers of
childhood are unique to each and unrecoverable in their full
intensity except through a scent, a glimpse of a half-recalled
landscape, a sound... Our Principal understood this and on
a sun-ridden day had no hesitation in closing books and
turning us out among long grass and cabbages to pick
Cabbage White caterpillars off the leaves. The background
of War assisted in the importance of the living moment ...*

May

Amongst wild garlic
under the alders
two of us sat –
my shadow longer than her's.

We stood: my shadow reached
across to the other bank –
sun striped the river.

The gnats were all about
and mayflies – a hatch of them
rising and falling, upright
with their long tails.

'Your hands are thin,
your skin shows through
like rice paper.'

She splayed her fingers
held them up. The sun
coloured them pink: they seemed
as fans, or the wings of young bats.

Strands

When she ran on to the terrace
her hands were palm down
as though to balance.
Her lips were thick –
her grey eyes gazed
from a colourless face.

The patter of bare feet –
a sun splashed dress –
twisted strands of wisteria
framed her as she knelt
at the table, her hand
cupping her chin.

Her face was hidden,
her black hair, a veil.
I watched her fingers
grasp a blunt pencil
force it to write.

*And always there was the moor. I was happy on it, its
emptiness didn't worry me although it was a lonely old
place, ghostly in wild weather, yet hard to imagine*

anything more joyous than following down a moor stream
in summer...

Larkbarrow

                        ...alone on the moor
a fine house ruined in a square of trees
its once magnificent drive grown over
black gaps served as windows in rotting frames
a chiselled portico enhanced the door.

In a gateway out of a let-go field
my pony pricked his ears. I felt him tense
sensed his anxiety,
stopped, as they say, in his tracks

I patted coaxed urged
looked round for a paper bag, an old cloth blowing,
a dead sheep –
the kind of thing that drives a horse silly

The gateway ahead of us hadn't changed
no gate swung between its posts –
I lead him, drew on the reins
extended his neck so I could see through

No change. No plank against the wall
no hurdle fallen – ears pricked, nostrils quivering
a frightened creature stood beside me
aware of something I couldn't see

Catching his fear I mounted, turned.
Larkbarrow loomed out of mist, sank back
its trees bent and whipped – an echo of hoofs

                                                followed

as we galloped. Stopped. The hoofs stopped later.

*One day my mother's radio was turned up louder than
I'd ever heard it. It was V. E. Day, the War in Europe
was over*

The Americans arrived...

                                with tanks in the village
halted beside the Green, directed the 'traffic',
handed out gum – the villagers cheered

They drove the road we walked to school,
crossed the ford. Up the lane above Liddycleave
they found a problem – the lane squeezed

Undeterred they drove their tanks

along the tops of the banks, marked them with tracks
like dogs against steps.

Surprised by shouts,
the increased incline, the drivers turned back,
left their imprint cut in rock.

*When Peace finally came with V. J. day, I stayed with a
school friend and we danced in the streets of Truro. I had
left childhood behind and was into puberty. In those days
childhood lasted much longer. I can honestly say that the
first time I registered looking at myself in the mirror was
at the age of eleven, because I had read Lorna Doone in an
old but fine copy with mould on it that I'd pulled out
of the cupboard. I longed to look like her only slightly
mildewed portrait on the cover...*

Girl Child

There was a happiness that ended in dream
or the long lost twilight of summer nights:
greenly it slid from behind foxglove candles
beside the child that circled its finger in sand.
Then the days rode on like dark waves in the

                                    moonlight

until eleven – the hour before midnight,
the hour I was adult, the afternoon
I lost the key in the river, flashing like mica
in the washed pebbles under a window of water.
I was sealed in my parents' envelope,
struggling into my personality like a glove,
holding tight to the broom-handle of childhood.
'You are a girl' they said, 'You are destined
for the mazy ways of houses – or great and bold
throw yourself around. Take on life.'
Then love sprang out of a thick bush
tore my dreams in tatters like Pyramus' lion.

*And so living on a hill farm on Exmoor ended for me in
1945 when my parents in spite of endeavouring to buy
Yealscombe were unable to, although they bought an
adjoining farm. Riscombe. But I never lived on the new
farm, so for me it wasn't the same and wasn't able to
conjure up the same intensity of memory.*

Dartmoor
1959–2004

Mist wraps round...

the house like a glove
steals over the bony knuckle of a hand
silence and more silence: in this fog
we live on an island without the sound of waves
in the distance a car hums along a road –
if we can break from this silence
and hear the helicopter above the cloud
we may still find where the breeze lifts
and the ground lies clear. Now I see them briefly
the pond, the trees, the high hard line
that marks the division of sky and moor –
put out your hand and pull me to you
for we are joined till one of us
drags off the glove.

By 1959 mechanisation had come to stay. Harry
Ferguson's invention of the hydraulic lift and the
machinery to go with it altered farming life slowly but
steadily from workers in the fields to the solo farmer with
his partner or wife managing between them – which is
what we had become by the 1990s. As the carthorse
became redundant so, by degrees and with rising wages,
did the labour force which was replaced by highly

*versatile contractors equipped with large tractors and
machinery.*

*We – Christopher and I with our three little boys –
arrived in June at Ford Farm, the best month of the year
on the moor, and took up our pitchforks. We had acquired
a Fordson tractor, a mower, and a buck-rake – the latter
hadn't arrived.*

Heat. Burning sun.
I wore a blue dress, I remember –
the children worked beside me
I rubbed sun-oil into their skins
sent them into the shade where the hedge curved over.
Lost in the dark doorway of the barn I heard them
                                    playing –
sweat ran down my face and into my mouth.

Then the men came, took my fork
turned the hay swathes with a natural methodical
                                    rhythm
almost a dance, it seemed as the heat rose in a wave
zig-zagged before my eyes.

*I think it was at this moment my past and present came
together – Exmoor and Dartmoor – because really the*

changes in hill farming were slight between the end of the
War and 1959, resulting in similar practices used on
Dartmoor to those I had known.

Previous to this we had been in Canada, the Southern
States of the USA and Swedish Llapland because
Christopher had been working in forestry.

The house stood as we had bought it. House sparrows
occupied the ivy, chirruped noisily, flew out in a swarm;
swallows swooped in and out of the old stables, long
grass, docks, and sorrel grew where we planned a lawn.
A leat was half buried, still water in a patch of reeds
suggested a pool beyond which was a high wire and
concrete fence. There were perches across the front porch
where chickens had roosted, and beneath stood a beehive
with honey-bees coming and going.

Janny, the previous owner, told us he was old, all of
55 – it was time to retire. I asked about the concrete posts,
the fence... 'Don't never touch they' he said, 'they's for the
fox. If you shift'em, he'll take th' hens.'

I absorbed the warning.

When Janny had moved into a bungalow we uprooted
the concrete posts, removed the wire, knocked down the
concrete dairy that was set in the front like a pill-box,
unearthed buried trash, old car wings, bedsteads and
springs, broken crockery, an enamel jug, holed saucepans –

*made a lawn and found a granite mounting block
against the yard wall.*

The fox took the hens one by one – we built a run.

*Up the central passage of the house I had to bend – I
was 5 ft 4 – Janny and Jim, the stockman, were built
like dwarfs with broad bent shoulders and bandy legs.
Janny's wife was tall and had presence – she seldom left
the house except for the garden and when we had come to
see the house she had been settled by the fire like ancient
stone, her kitchen was like a long low cave built into the
hill. A fireplace was halved with a stove in front of it, a
tree trunk lay in the grate smoking. The room was dark
but fine, it had sold us the house for the only other was
the parlour with black oppressive shutters and a black
Victorian fireplace surrounded by mottled tiles.*

*Upstairs were two rooms and a bathroom with rotten
boards – the rest was lofts, also with plenty rotten boards.
The north wing over the kitchen was laid out with apples
We had wondered if the house would be big enough but
were in no position to fuss – we went in one bedroom, the
children in the other – it was quite simple. It was all
nicely swept and clean.*

*Fortunately when we first saw Ford it was summer
because it is doubtful if even we, young and idealistic
with a family to house, would have bought it in winter.*

*We were really amazingly naive – or I was. We sat on
the moor above the farm and looked down on it – it
'looked nice,' was affordable and came with a cottage,
plus an existing stockman willing to work with us. Above
all Christopher had liked the land and thought he could
make a living from it which was of prime importance.
Dartmoor was then an area where land was cheap. The
moor rose on either side and I felt it my friend. Open.
I could see to distant hills. In those early years I walked
over it a lot, and later with the children.*

Lines on Now – and Then

These trees hang still as a backdrop.
No leaf shifts – even the air threatens.
Crows scuffle on the roof, caw from beeches:
we live on an island of grey cut off from sun,
await wind to clear a path
through matted cloud.

A bird's whistle breaks the silence,
see-saws doubtfully out of nothing,
dies unanswered. I turn through a gate
of darkness to an owl's hoot.
Dawn. The leat's trickle

cries up from underground.
The house assumes life: a door opens,
stairs creak, footsteps, voices –
a kettle's hum: the cat stretches, yawns,
slinks from the bed.

We urban children grew
under slipper leaves of rhododendron
crawled on hands and knees
through undergrowth, paddled
in a goldfish pool in the box circle,
built stick houses in ghost trees.
Our bare feet pattered along terraces,
dodged the twirling hose sprinkling rose-beds,
picnicked on pine-needles
under tall trees

In the dry belt
shade was our river, flickering,
dabbling shadow: insects pestered,
hornets hummed, mosquitoes drilled
in the long hot evenings
under muslin screens.

Moving west brought the passion
of water, keeping pace, running

beside us as we darted downward
following the stream that turned to river
leaping, jostling, urging us
scratched and sliding, on and on
towards the flat plains, to loop
in pools under sallow and willow,
spread in a widening smile
along the calm of the estuary
until its mouth met sea's salt lips
lapping in ripples,
jerking roughened waves,
absorbed the sinuous body
of river into ocean's tide

Creeping past the smell
of pungent mud-flats, past
thin-legged waders under a lead sky;
we turned inland over water-meadows
trod slimy planks stretched
across reed beds, dodged cattle
grazing in emerald

Out of nowhere came swifts
wings set, diving, gliding, rising,
gleaning insects, clustering, twittering

darting on holed sandbanks
flanking flat-lands

Free of the river's guidance
entering woods, darkened
in the dusk of evening,
dampening under misty rain,
obscuring sight,
silencing chatter to mount
through a twilight of alder
into a spruce plantation
guarding its edge
with branches spiked as needles.
The sinking sun painted clouds
lit the sombre face of darkness

Wet tarmac striped the up-lands,
white grass stirred on road's shoulders:
we longed for a generator's hum –
the boisterous flash of a one-armed bandit
the smoked heat of burning peat.

Smoke blurred the barman
voices merged in noise, warmth
cuddled like friendly hands.

Dartmoor · 1959–2004

Sliding along varnished benches
imbibing the blousy smell of ale,
we turned our pockets out for coins –
waited dumbed by human contact

Outside the long road
stretches silver centred:
black-face sheep hunch in lumps
under headlights' stare –
a passing rush of air
carrying diesel spoils
night's silence. Moonlight
dodges cloud, ridges of tinners'
workings cast shadow in deep gullies
rising irregularly, leading down
to the valley floor
cut by a snake white stream

Chimneys mount against the sky:
lights flare in disparate windows
polishing cobbles. A figure moves:
the lights go out: we stand alone.
Casting off boots on flagstones,
calling upstairs
we drop on chairs, sprawl

demanding attention
clumsy as wet dogs
shaking off water.

*I put my shoes on the floor in Ford, found them two weeks
later covered in mould. My father came to see us and
kindly gave us a present of central heating which was,
and still is, the best present we ever had.*

*I will describe the plan of Ford in some detail because
I find it interesting, and because I think any observations
of old houses of a classic pattern should be recorded,
especially if changes are made. The couple before us had
lived at Ford for twenty five years, so it was not a house
that changed hands quickly as so many do when the land
is not adequate to support a house and family. Its land,
with Easdon the adjoining farm (for which we sold
Ford's cottage a few years later in order to buy) makes
our land amount to 264 acres; of that about 64 is woods
or rough marsh grazing and undoubtedly a very good
habitat for wildlife. About 70 acres is first class hay or
arable land, and the rest good grazing pasture. As hill
farms go it is – or was – big enough to make a living.*

*The house is built of moor-stone granite with a
cobbled cross passage through its centre. It bears a
resemblance to the Exmoor farmhouse I lived in through*

*the War, but Ford with its ancient cobbled yard, fine
granite piggeries, bee boles, and other granite features
remains superior both historically and from the point of
view of a home. Upstairs it is rambling and quite
minimally altered in plan except for the conversion of an
adjoining 'linney' into three children's rooms. It seems
likely that its most ancient part (probably where the
existing living room and office is now) had a central
hearth, as the oldest timbers in the roof of that end only
are blackened, and it was cut off upstairs in '59 from
both the shippen beneath and central passage by a thick
wall. This suggests it was the site of a dwelling well
before the 16/17th century plan it now follows and would
substantiate the mystifying claim by the previous owners
that parts of it were said to go back some 900 years.*

*On the ground floor, which literally is the ground, it
follows the plan of a classic moor longhouse with yard
and buildings demonstrating the well thought out design
of the ancient farm where everything was placed for ease
and convenience in the feeding of animals in a severe
climate. Cattle and humans shared the same roof using a
common entrance but divided from their stock by a central
passage. The shippen half had a hayrack along the wall
and included a pig salting bath (now outside), the
central or through-passage supported pig-rollers between*

its joists for bleeding pigs, the gentle slope of the cobbles
beneath making it easy to swill out afterwards...

    The ash house a little way off, is a small round
building with a conical-shaped corbelled roof. I am told
ashes were put in it from the fires to prevent danger to the
original thatch, and make use of as fertiliser to spread on
the fields, but I have never met anyone who could tell me
categorically that was *its purpose.*

Hill Farm '59

The builders took the slates off,
went away, said they'd be back
next day. The old kitchen
stood like a tired horse,
walls rose at the apex
like thin withers
sticking out of bony ribs –
the old table, too big to move
sagged in the centre.

Awe-struck at the skeleton,
my own form heavy with child
we watched in hope under
the summer sky, ate outside

77

in a yard piled high
with cement bags, tools, wheelbarrows –
junk subsiding in heaps.

The storm came out of nowhere,
lightning forked the night –
thunder fumbled, struck
and seemed to shake the house.
Wind slammed doors, rain
sluiced the quarry tiles
washed them pristine
as pebbles in a clear stream.
Sun flickered a glint off mica
as the builder's lorry
entered the yard.

Voices called above
banging and drilling, a chink
of china, cups of tea.
Life muttered in the old building –
the old slates replaced
closed over like a lid.
The new-lit stove
bubbled and gurgled in unison
with the new-born child.

Ford was thatched until a few years before we bought it. Janny, who had purchased it at the end of the first World War when many farms were sold off at special dispensation to the existing tenant farmers, had applied for a grant to re-thatch but the grant advisor did not turn up to see it by the specified date, so Janny who had no love of thatch removed the existing dilapidated thatch and slated it. I asked Mrs Ash who had worked at Ford and helped looked after the house when needed, what Ford was like thatched? Her answer was 'Dirty old stuff, one time I come down, it had been proper dry, then a shower come and the roof was covered in rats, I don't know how many, hundreds of 'em. They was living in it and come out for the water.' Apart from this story I'm rather glad Ford isn't still thatched. It is a fact that a great many of the old farms with thatched roofs sooner or later burn down. Certainly the ritual of a faggot made of ash and bound with hazel ties to burn on Christmas Eve would have been ill-advised – and a loss because every time a tie gives on the faggot the company must drink.

We continued discovering new things about the house over the years...

A spring...

        rose in winter
trickled from the back wall
down through the kitchen
washed the pitted quarry tiles
lapped the fire-bricks
crept round the table
unmoved because immovable.

When the waters subsided
we stood each table-leg in tanalith,
sighed –
even the table was not immutable.

Though sitting at dinner
it had seemed immortal –
and we the flecks in the sunbeam
that slid through the window
swam in the darkness, floated up
and as the sun shifted,
died.

Two other ancient farms make up Ford's land. Once separate
holdings, both have long since ceased to function as dwellings;
one, Canna, is in regular use for stock handling and shelter;
the other, Cripdon, is set as is Ford, on what we have been told

was the main track/lane to Ashburton that went up past the mediaeval ruins of Blissmoor (corruption of the ancient Anglo-Saxon Bliche's mor: OED) over Cripdon Down and joined the existing road beneath Jay's Grave. This is marked as a track on the Ordnance Survey map of 1888. Beside it in our fields are well defined hut circles and an ancient leat running from Blissmoor to Cripdon, presumably made by tinners.

This same track had a fork off to the left shortly after Cripdon with a stoned base, stepping stones, clapper and further bridge that led to the adjoining Tor Hill Farm. It is marked as a 'track' on the Ordnance Survey map of 1888, but is wide enough and well enough bottomed to have been used by a horse and cart. These farms were of necessity small in acreage being usually run by one family of tenant farmers only able to feed and shelter a restricted amount of stock. Cripdon (Crippon) is on the opposite side of the valley from Ford, and is reached by crossing the Hayne Brook that runs off Hameldown and separates the two valleys. It is believed to be the original ford used before there was a bridge and road built at Ford Gate, and is said to date from Saxon times...

Sand curves like a fin
under flood-water's thrust –
water swirls my boots

the current drags sideways.
I step from water to more water
pushing a path
between mud and sticks

Hazel leans from the banks –
wind bows the tops of alder
that give and straighten
whiplash back

Cattle cower along the hedge
wet as seals
accepting their houseless lot –
ruffled birds see-saw
snowdrop petals lift like wasp-wings

Sky blues in a lull –
sun steams the land

*

In the ruined mediaeval buildings that line the lane
nettles grow to the height of walls –
an elder tree in summer burdened by white blossom
in autumn becomes dark berries tinged scarlet
dangling on maroon stalks for scavenging birds

*

Ghost Children

There is no time to sigh
beside the cold dark walk:
neither you nor I
will bend to wash hands
in the pool's still surface
dabbed by gnats: only the children
walking from their ruined home to church
laugh down the lane with voices
young as the day they died –
or simply ceased to pass
from stepping stone to stone
over pool and grass
where mayfly rose to dance,
the water of the ford
too low to stir
held a mirror up to limbs
thin as the sallow's branch.
that closes in.
The silence after
of fertile sidling hedges
anticipates shared laughter –
settles on the empty
sunlight of the yard.

*In the early years at Ford my occupation was twofold –
looking after the three little boys to whom a daughter was
soon added, and painting which I did in a barn loft. It
was all right in summer but very cold in winter; even so I
appreciated the space and skylights. As my paintings were
abstract and abstract painting was unheard of then except
by a few, and was generally derided, I used to carry them
into the house faced towards me preferably draped in a
blanket! – although at the time they were on the circuit
of major exhibitions.*

*On the farm, I was mainly necessary to translate for
Christopher the Devon dialect of the knowledgeable old
stockman we had inherited, perhaps because I had grown
up amongst a similar tongue. Otherwise there was
plenty of labour to be had and wages at the time were
ridiculously low. But living on a farm you inevitably
become a part of it; I learnt to drive the tractor early on –
it takes two people to pull a tractor out of a bog – and I
was also a taker of messages delivered by person or phone
and which often meant searching the farm to find where
work was taking place, usually where the land was being
reclaimed. It was on one of these errands I was witness to
the Trackscavator working – a straggling yellow
machine, the predecessor of today's Digger.*

The Trackscavator...

crashed into scrub and tore up hedges
seized gateposts in steel teeth, thrust them aside
lifted old flagstones in Crippon yard.
I stood shivering at the destruction
my heart bled for the old, shrank from change
Boulders were unearthed, carried across fields
thrown into rough ground down by the stream.

A farm had to have fields, boulders prevented
                                        cultivation
it was logic but alien – the loss of topsoil –
old Jim was nearly in tears
at the ruthless insistence of machines
the disturbance of ground he'd walked over
for twenty-five years –
and everywhere wire.

Clearing Thorn

The Digger came, blocked
the gate, blundered a path
across a bog, burst
through a crumbling bank.

Thorn spread in woven chain-mail mesh
birds twittered down spiked alleys.
The Digger lowered claws
shovelled the spilled-over thicket
tearing and ripping, receding
and advancing, encroaching
in an elephantine dance.
Bit by bit yellow teeth
heaped the cruel thorn
watched by a farmer
craving the last longed-for acre
out of dishevelled waste.

Sparks
shot like fireworks
into the twilit sky.
The Digger rootled and prised
for buried boulders, smoothed ruffled earth,
drew blunt fingers
over a cowed land.

*I implored for the granite posts to be replaced wider apart,
usually to no effect. Wood posts are easier, and replacing
granite takes time and costs more. Large machinery*

inevitably meant wider gateways and fields without boulders. Granite gateposts were more often seen lying alongside the banks than used for their original purpose; as a result the ends of the walls fell out because it was the granite posts that had held them in place. During recent years the National Park Authorities are making an effort to maintain them, but in many cases the gateways remain so narrow it simply precludes entry. On some farms numerous hedges were removed making a first unaware step against bird life, as did the spraying of fields round the headlands to kill weeds. Even banks were sprayed leaving nowhere for the wild strawberries and raspberries and uncountable species of grasses and wildflowers that grow in them.

Ford's land on either side runs up to moor – to the north rises the conical pointed form of Easdon, to the south Cripdon Down leads to Swine Down and on to Hound Tor. Across the valley to the west is the high moor ridge of Hameldown acting as a rain umbrella. In summer in the hay fields it often seems that rain clouds are coming causing general panic, but mostly the clouds stay curling back over Hameldown and don't cross the valley, menacing but not invading.

Shadows paint indigo stripes
massing darkness under the ridge: sun dusts a

                                                fine line

inked between moor and sky

Mist rolls forward extending furtive fingers
to clasp the abundant heather: bracken droops

                                            feather arms

like dancers on a raked stage.

Sleeping cattle loom
their licked hides bloom like gem-stones set in gold:
tree leaves shiver at the sudden onslaught of

                                            crude weather

Oh I am wrapped in it, it's reached me now
caught my cheeks with dull wet kisses: I submit

                                            with frightened joy

to a strange communion
the intimacy of mist and heather.

*I was frequently used for assistance in finding and driving
back escaped animals such as the hill sheep we shared with
the neighbouring farmer to use our moor Grazing Rights
(the right to graze a certain section of moor according to*

the farm deeds). These rights, with the later acquisition
of Easdon farm adjoining Ford to the north, stretched to
the Warren House on the Postbridge road, and were also
used by cattle and ponies...

He stood on the rocks and shouted –
the cattle came over the skyline
one by one leaning into the wind
heads lowered – Charolais, Devon,
Friesian-Angus cross, all together
battled towards him, moved round the hill
in a frieze – hya hya hya – advancing
in a long fine trickle.

The sky's gone birds-eye blue
above undulating backs wending
in slow methodic rhythm –
hya hya hya
O strange wild call
knocked off a mountain face
or sung by Mary over quickening sands.

That first summer stretched obligingly on...

I lived as a star-eyed fool loving you –

thistles smashed as you swung around the field
in your old blue beat-up tractor –
I had to run ahead of you
to get the white ducks out of the Yellow-rattle.
When you came back for a fill of diesel
the tractor juddered like a live thing,
a horse over-ridden: it shook and shook –
fumes from the exhaust smudged the tree leaves
into undulating water weed,
even the gate-lex pulsed like idle fish.

I followed the geometric print of wheels
over hot tarmac into the fields,
sank into the moist refuge of bank
my feet in white clover singing with bees.

Brown summer...

                    of brittle grass
stretching in balding ridges
where cattle thirst for the last siphoned drop
seeping imperturbably into the hastily bought trough

The pond has sunk to a mud-hole,
stream water lies in stasis to the sun –
at midday there is a holy silence
of pooled cattle in a hot wind.
Eyes flow at the corners besieged by flies
their solemn faces watch but cannot stir the burnt land
smouldering under slotted feet
Should I become intercessor
beg growth from a noon stillness of fields
grazed to naked earth.

*During our second year we acquired a forage harvester and
invested in a Harvestore tower with a Kondskilde blower –
the former for cutting and picking up grass for silage as
well as assisting in the clearance of bracken, and the latter
for the storage of corn...*

Barley...

      heads ripen as evenly
as a girl's plaited hair –
its long antennae bow and rise
snatched by wind
The combine enters – large, yellow,
blatant, squats like a bull frog –.

the driver smokes, takes stock, studies the

                                              gold corn

rising to crown the hill

Starts his engine, sits up front.
A roar of sound, the beat of the spinning bed
as it batters down the field's centre
ruthlessly reaping the valued crop
filling its tank

Waits

The driver screws a thick neck over his shoulder

A tractor and trailer pull out, approach the

                                     impatient combine,
drive alongside, receive the winnowed grain –
a satisfactory gold-horde grows

Beside the tower the trailer tips
slides barley through its hatch –
grain swirls, sucked, blown
hissing up the pipe
mounts the twenty-foot height
to an opened mouth –

grain rains on the tower's floor

This entire process from crop in the field to crushing was acted out and filmed by the BBC in 1983, and networked in '84 and '85 featuring Cheryl Campbell in a three part series I wrote about a hill farm entitled 'A Winter Harvest'. The tower remains but sadly unused because with the removal of government subsidies, the hill farms could no longer compete with lowland farms and it became cheaper to buy in barley for feed.

Canna, the other deserted farm on our land, consists of an old cottage, not lived in since the 19th century or even earlier, and mainly known for its association with the Jay's Grave myth (see William Crossing's Guide to Dartmoor*) It provides a fine yard used for handling stock, a great barn and various useful buildings – including an added 'crush' (or 'race') for handling cattle and a foot bath for sheep.*

We bought a Hereford bull and crossed it with a variety of cows. But when the stockman was found taking refuge up a tree, we sold it. Later we were to settle for a young Charolais bull, white and lively. He had to be walked from his home to Ford which was no easy matter – he was a forceful character and walked through gates as though they weren't there. But generally he was reasonable and not at all aggressive. Called Storm he became the backbone of our herd...

The white bull...

> burst into the garden
the gate rose on his neck in a shatter of iron
twisted out of frame. He trampled over leeks
and rubbed against the apple tree –
a branch fell on his cream hide.
He drove against the wall like a sea roller
battering with the poll of his head –
in a blunder or sunken hooves
he heaved from the earth,
brambles dragged behind him in traces
smoothing the trench of his walk.
Pausing, he took stock of the ruled plot
the figures that closed in.

Sorting cattle

Wind groans in the sycamores at Canna

a corrugated roof clatters in an iron gust –
dung sucks at boots slithering in a sea of slime
each foot freed with a plunk

Big eyed calves in the 'crush' gaze
wedged between bars: soulful mothers lift
bellowing heads to the ' gate.'

The bull saunters into the yard like the police –
In a ripple of muscle and red rimmed eyes he takes
                                                          stock

We clutch our sticks like straws
funnelled up before a tornado

*Autumn hedge-trimming is usually done by a
contractor but sometimes by the farmer himself. When we
were first on the farm the banks were maintained and the
hedges cut and laid because there was still the labour to
do it, but since the '70s or earlier hedges have been
trimmed mechanically by a farmer or a contractor.*

*The Environmentally Sensitive Areas are now attempting
to return the farms to the old fashioned method including
the earthing up of banks, but done with machinery. It
seems a good idea except for the immense amount of wire
needed to protect the banks' sides from stock rubbing them
out – perhaps if more money was put into walling instead
of wire it might prove more lasting...*

Hedge Trimmer

Rain washes
scattered black ash leaves –
trimmed thorn
waits to spike.

A scarred hedge cringes
showing gashed stems –
the clanking mutilation
repeats and repeats its devastation.

Sticks spin
flung up by blades –
the change of tone,
the crunch as the trimmer eats the sides

decapitates
the leading shoots,
equals out the chances
of proud trees larking with the sky.

The ford runs low...

                       after a parched summer
its peat-brown water huddles leaves round its edge –
wrinkles of scum line its looking-glass face.

I cross by a single stone up a dried lane
beside stepping stones grown over –
the goose and gander race to meet me.
From behind the blue tractor
in the dark of the donkey house
a man's face glows as he bends over a wheel,
prises it, holds it down with his boot.

Tonight he will fold me in arms thick as trees
his knees like angle iron will slot into mine –
an amalgamation of limbs rooting for life.

The farmer...

        plods in cuffed gum-boots
slashing at brambles straggling gates
grubbing out grass clods grown at foot
clearing – cleaning – mending
digging out ditches – freeing drains

He is the land's keeper
the field-husband
the restraint in a dance
of impassioned growth

The humble animals pay their due –
weaned – fed – sheltered
tested and injected,
only to be slaughtered before their time.

*Now steers (castrated bulls) must be sold for meat before 30
months; before BSE* (Bovine spongiform encephalitis) *they would have been kept till 2 years or more to gain their
full potential.*

Fog holds the hills...

gathers round the house
like hands in a death clasp.

I am half afraid of it – its insidious grip.
Up in the fields I call the cows.
Silence and more silence.
Then out of the grey-clothed fields
the Blue-roan bellows.

No sign of her.

The ring-feeder shows steel uprights,
its bed a mound of left-over seeds
waits for this year's bales.
I cut the string, shake each apart,
listen for the slow tread, the dull thump
of head against another's rump.
In ones and twos they emerge
calves trailing, plunge moist heads
through bars, jerk and pull
strenuous in desire

Their rhythmic munch calms.

*A regular happening in autumn on the moor used to be the
pony drift or round-up. Every farmer who had ponies
helped, either riding or on foot, to bring them off the
Commons (the moor) for sorting. Generally the best mares
are kept on with a stallion and the others sold at the pony*

*sales. In recent years, owing to no longer being able to
transport ponies live across the Channel, the price has
dropped so much that farmers can't afford to keep them.
Visitors don't quite realise the extra work and cost to keep
moor ponies healthy through the winter and, like everything,
if it doesn't pay ultimately they have to go. There is now a
plan to reintroduce them as they help the vegetation, and are
a tourist draw. Tourism has become the main industry
bringing more income to the area than anything else,
although the long-term benefits are debatable.*

Pony Drift

Over the bare top of the high moor
ponies pour – mares, yearlings, suckers,
bays and coloureds crush the turning bracken –
cracks and shouts startle a lark
tucked in grass.

At the gateway
rippling flesh swirls, thins to undulating backs
pounding down a narrow lane.

Horsemen bound over the misted ridge
trap the scared ponies –

picked out, thrown, sat on,
ear-marked,
sorted.

At the sales
hot eyes and crater nostrils distend
as the hammer falls on tomorrow

Bidders' lips moisten on the ring rail.

Grazing Rights

'See here' he said, 'we've come about the ponies.'
The two of them stood outside in the yard
one with his knee up on the wall, the other
by the gate: trouble rode their slouch
like a hard man on a donkey.
The Commoner cocked a keen eye:
'Whose are these ponies up on top the Down?
We want them off. If they're not yours
it isn't legal.' Eagerly he stared at me
as though to fix my eye on him
like a chicken's beak to chalk.

'We share them – share them with a friend.'
Sam was three score and ten, no longer quick
to get about – and now these men
were come to hound him, chase him off the Down
like snapping whippets.

'He's no more ponies up there than we've got Rights.'
'Aye, but you can't go letting' em' –
the Commoner spoke up bold. 'It was sharing,' I said
'not letting.' He shook his head and rubbed it.
The other blinked ferret eyes,
'You'd better put it right or we'll get the stick.'

When Sam brought out his bales to feed the ponies,
he found strangers with a camera taking photos,
slinking about our Common like furtive dogs.
There was no law I knew that could prevent them.
'What'll you do, Sam?' I asked him.
'Sell'em – the prices is good.'
They were sold that week in the local market,
mares, suckers, horse-ponies, all went for meat.
It heralded the end of neighbourly feeling
when Grazing Rights were shared by people.

The winters of the '60s and '70s began with cold autumns,
the temperature often dropping sharply over night bringing
white frost... It is on these dark evenings that
most of us resent our isolation, long for bright lights and
all that goes with them. Such a place came briefly to
Dartmoor – it seemed too good to be true...

A Club rose over the hill – a large Victorian
            house with gables lifting out of trees
            in spear-heads, psycho-esque.
Locals gathered, hung about the bar slap-
            happy over their pint. Girls emerged
like moths from chrysalis, wrapped poppy
            pink and scarlet-beaded shawls
            around bare shoulders, lived the night
forgot the day in gum-boots searching fields
            for last year's ewe with this year's lamb

The clientele increased. Saturday nights we
            stole out, left children with a sitter –
            'So near, such a gift! Just over the hill.'
The Club's fame glowed above the angular
            lantern – shady, brazen, inviting...
            'Anyone who was anyone' was there

standing round looking. just looking,
      touching their hair...

      'Annabel's' one night 'Dick's' the next –
the London crowd came – people in other rooms
      with other voices, other tunes – played
      snooker, the juke-box, one-eyed bandits,
danced to disco lights. The regulars sat
      at a long Formica table
      played 'Black Jacks', drank –
money shuffled hands. 'Anyone who was anyone'
      was there, standing round looking,
      just looking, touching their hair...

Shining Mercs parked between dung-spattered
      pick-ups, canvas-hooded vans
      nestled among foliage.
The brawling came after closing – a Club could
      close late, Dick said. It was Dick they
      came for, Dick the charmer with see-all
eyes and wits sharp as a blade. Fights. Rumours
      spread like rancid butter – with a knife.
      'Anyone who was anyone' was there
standing round looking, just looking ...

The police invaded the Country Club in the trees,
        closed it down. It vanished like a precious
        ear-ring slipped from an ear to disappear
in heather – not like the bomber crashed on
        the moor above, still showing a scar.

Dartmoor returned to silent, moderately sober normality –
it was winter.

Minus ten...

  the ice cringes
cracks splay out like sun on glass.
Tentatively I step back –
glazed spears surround me.
A cow ambles to the peacocks tail
of water where the stream
joins the pond, skids and slithers,
one hoof penetrates the surface
thin as fat on cold gravy,
sinks to the knee, lurches
drags out each muddied limb
reaches, touches its ringed
reflection, blows steaming breath
drinks in long rhythmic gulps.

A magpie perches on a frozen molehill
awaiting the undigested barley
dropped in dung: its Prussian
plumage shines: its bill
drills fractured earth.
The drinking cow lifts her head
water drips from her steaming muzzle
above a still-born skin that lies discarded,
past disguise of the fostered offspring.
Wide mouthed as a gargoyle
the calf staggers in the gateway.
Cold closes her fist.

*Certainly winters with short days, low light, and long
hours indoors can cause depression – or Lapp sickness, as
it's called – and seem interminable. Up until the late
'70s there were still days of snow, sun, and the clear cold
air that came with it. We see little of that now...*

Excerpt from **'A Local Tale'**

She bends by the fire,
takes up bellows
fans the frail flame –
when she stops blowing,

it drops down –
nothing but a hiss.

*

Ear-rings swaying
she descends the stairs
'Where are you going?'
'I'd like to go out' she said
'Could we go out?'
'What do you want to go out for.
What's wrong with here?'
'Nothing, it's just I want a change.'
Through the window the moon
floated in a halo of haze –
'We could go to the White Hart.'
'You go' he said, 'I'll stay here.'

The winds came, tore trees,
ripped branches, tossed slates,
piled up leaves in drifts.
Birds flitted along the shelter
of the house, huddled in bushes
white crocus stood stiff
as bridesmaids waiting for sun –
early lent lilies bobbed

broodies smothered
the rooster's tail blew sideways.

Chickens pecked lime
from the wall, ducks squeezed
under the gate, rolled
like sailors down to the pond –
fog slid down the valley,
circled the church, spread
like a shroud.

'I'll go tomorrow, I've got to
sort things out' she said.
He was leaning on the wall
grappling with a bolt.
Inside the house on the stairs
she watched dust dance
under the skylight:
her hand slid up the bannister –
so old it was and polished
brown and round, quite
without sharp edges.

Spring threw off winter
like a white lace shawl –

bones emerged on grass,
washed bare: a blinded
sheep blunders with crow-pecked
eyes, her lambs wriggle
in an ecstasy of milk.

Easter came early,
the altar bare. In the window
Mary stood in blue with the child
by her side and Joseph behind:
glass fragmented and spun
in reds and blues and greens.

She has not gone: the bed
is warmer now, needs
less blankets. Spreading
her arms she went to the meadow
where the stream curls along the hedge
like a tress of hair: she washed
her face in ice-cold water,
paddled the stream's bed

Sun came in May
cascading through conker leaves
on to mown grass. She sat in smocks

and shadow waiting for the life
that stirred, her head laid back
in dream as the swallows dived
through the broken pane
and martins glued
nests to the eaves

Then the birth in the night
and the morning star
that slipped down the hill
to the launderers' pool,
and the rooster's call
that mixed with the cry
from the bed where the mother
laboured: until he came
and bent his head to look
at his child in a blanket of blue.

And the days went on
in a different way.

The cruel month

Snow – mid April, falling fast.
White rooves. Black and sienna doors.

No birds. Only the cock crows.

My cat purrs warm beside me,
black-blotched head, black-tailed,
the rest white on white

on the duvet stripes. My hand
nestles the fur of her soft stomach
her head lies against me

till I heave, slide out into iced air
see the trees behind the barn
have turned to hills of dappled grey.

The bullocks lie under trees
in their whitened field, flatten
kidney prints under hot bodies –

their muzzles drip:
one trails a string of saliva
transparent as water

its chocolate cheeks chew
beneath poll and ears dusted in snow
like sifted flour.

My boots print through
leave a single trail lost in
emerald under spears of fur –

a bough has split off, crashed
lies in a mess of smashed limbs
among spiked needles.

Inside the house I open the stove's lid
lean over the flat round plates
breathing in warmth

open the oven door, luxuriate
in the hot blast of air, splay
shrunk-fingered gloves like bats' wings.

*Our sheep usually lambed in the fields and were
immediately brought in to a building. Foxes take lambs
regularly if they are left out. In the spring of '71
Christopher went to Colombia for 6 weeks prospecting for
a company in search of gold. On my own with the
stockman who was living at Easdon with his family,
times became hard. The lambing went well on the frost
frozen ground – I can remember going out to bring in new-
born lambs in the unforgettable clarity of the freezing*

nights. We finished with approximately 200 ewes and
lambs and the cold continued into mid-April. The hay
ran out and the sheep took over, no field contained them so
I sold them – fortunately for a good price!

Moon

I shut the window,
close out the greenish
silver of moon, the shining
silence of pond.

No duck stirs, no goose
honks in violation of night's perfection.
The whole earth waits
with its face turned away
from the baked burn of sun.

It's the cold globe holds
the power of passivity,
draws the sea, the Spring
and Neap, the peeling back
of water from sand
like a skin.

As a ghost might
guide a hunter, moon's unreality,
her dark body seen only in reflection –
stirs primate depths.

*There was no light pollution then. Now, in 2004, there
is light pollution from the towns glowing to the south and
east, also from flashing beams for horse protection – light
is believed to inhibit the roosting of wild birds...*

Gale in January

Larches lie scarred across the cleave
knocked flat by a gone-mad wind.
Contorted roots clutch at air.

New-born boulders lodge above a crater's womb –
two upright sentinels of knobbled oak
sprout twigs like ill-shaven men.

A jack-knifed juggernaut of ash
lies crashed across the path –
a pile-up of young trees blocks the leat.

Bluebells will pattern the needles' rug –

crested-wrens call like rusty hinges –
Buzzards mew their loss.

Veil

Wind blasts at eaves –
a metal chimney rocks.

Jackdaws chuck: doves huddle on gutters
ruffled by wind's rage.

Small birds hurtle past like bullets.

The cat balls herself into the quilt.

I watch the bouncing cherry branches
lift a veil of white lace

The holly tree...

                    lay in a tangled mass
tethered by branches, trapped by a trunk
grey coated and solid as a fallen man

its pristine flesh showed white
where the chain-saw sliced it
clean as a plate

sprung twigs clutched
the body from which they were sawn
muddied, trammelled, unwillingly dragged
to a heap, resistant to the last

Overnight the deer came
elegant slots marked the mud
holly lay savaged, strewn,
glossy leaves curled
pale with dying

The chain-saw deafened. Logs rolled free
exposing torn boughs

Spring

stiff shoots sprang from the bole
young leaves unfurled
soft as flesh of the new-born.

Most of our cattle used to calve in March making it the most exhausting and testing time of year because the climate can be diabolic – cold, wet, ice, driving snow or rain. Freezing winds. And with birth almost inevitably in a big herd come troubles. Our herd gradually built up to 84 calving cows – they lived out on the moor till after Christmas and then came in to the fields for feeding. In bad weather conditions they came off the moor earlier and any cow getting near to calving would be kept in the fields beside the buildings. Spring fortunately brings with it the relief of light mornings and longer evenings. On the moor such things assume an importance that can pass unnoticed in the city.

The following 'calving' poems make it seem as though calves repeatedly die in birth, but it is simply that the most traumatic moments fix in the mind – a happy outcome to a birth usually entails going home to breakfast! In the extreme cold of spring mornings at 5 a.m., if you are not present at the moment of birth the calf can become too cold to stand and suck. It may be asked, Why not calve in a building? But cows that normally live out are generally happier and more likely to calve successfully in the field – few farmers have not sat up at night reviving a half frozen calf or lamb by the ovens heat...

The calving cow strains...

a slime-black calf ejects.
Crooning she slobbers over
the mucus cauled mound,
her rasping tongue massages
the life pulse, nudges up
the creature squeezed out
like tar, abhorrent
in its devil stage, yellow-nosed
cloven-hoofed, hound-headed,
born hand in hand with death.

Night birth

Water filled prints
ruts in slush
wind torn rows
of littered boughs

Dawn's grey hills
white quilted fields
torch beams trace
the cleave's face

Cattle shapes loom
a calf sucks –
a mother eats
after-birth skin

stretched thin

Still-born

They were all up there pulling off a calf:
the cow had been down but was up
trampling round in the thorn.
'We'll get her in the building' one said
'So as us can get up close.'
The mad-eyed cow, head down, staggered
among the rough stone and went down in

the corner.
They got a rope round the calves feet sticking

out cold –
the tongue was out too, swollen, the calf

was dead.
Three of them pulled it off, laid it out.
'A big calf,' they said, 'Best ring for the hunt.'

Twin calf

Like a braised joint
laid out on the floor,
breathing uneasily, cold in the mouth
– a low hard ba-ah ejaculated
prematurely from the lungs, a sound
dragged up from underground

Then the breathing ceased,
the twin-calf lay inert,
eye unresponsive, tongue protruding.
You pumped and it breathed –
you stopped and it stopped
(like a game of grandmother's footsteps)
air expired with a slight disturbance,
a quiver, a sigh of flesh

A tube went down to its stomach
of glucose and water – then poured
from its nostrils and dripped
on the slates – its lungs were
squelching pockets of rain
that worked in and out
like a blacksmith's bellows

You lifted it up and carried it out –
it flopped in the wheelbarrow
like a toy in a store,
a long-limbed calf
with a yellow-nosed grin –
dead, you said.

Death of a Cow

The dead cow lies on her side:
her calf stands loath
to leave the mother who rose
to feed until the last,
floppy uddered, useless, sad –
the ultimate defeat –
carted to the knacker's yard

Coarse hands pull apart
functions fine-tuned
that kept life going on –
peritonitis, septicaemia of the heart –
post-mortem done.

May makes a wreath of white
to shock life from earth's meal of bone.

Armed

Rain slops from gutters
splashes non-stop on soggy ground:
wind trumpets from the east

Hunched cattle line the banks
glinting crystal raindrops on their hides
their fetlocks sunk in dung

The gateway's mud grips –
I hold the post, with my free hand
ease out the caught boot

Each step slides out behind.
I brave the open field to find a calf
shrunk between bank and fallen boulder

slap it, try to get it up –
the mother comes charging
stops, legs braced, head down

I stand aside to let her have a go.
She licks it, moos and croons
casts me a candid eye

pneumonia – I walk away.
She bellows – she's no fool, she knows
her calf is sick and I the healer.

Indoors I sterilise the syringe –
spike the bottle-top
drag up the fluid.

Armed, I force the door
go out to treat it.

The singling or felling of trees in woodland, or of felling
trees dangerously overhanging buildings, is a frequent
necessity that goes with farming. In this area trees grow
with such speed and mature so quickly, especially ash and
sycamore, that the need to fell comes up frequently...

Tree Fellers

The wall cornered beneath the sycamore
the tree forked, the one leant over the power-
lines, wall and house – the other rose
waving its wing-formed twigs to rooks,
crows, starlings and passing cloud.

Two men coiled the rope and checked the winch
the taller slung the chain-saw on his back
the other flung a rope over a fork
knotted a loop. One foot in a stirrup
the first went up the tree.

At the fork he walked out on the bough.
Fearful beneath we watched him balance –
'It's rotten' I called out. 'So it is' –
he grinned indifferent as the bouncing sky
then jerked the chain-saw cord till it sang
                                    with noise.

He caught another branch and leaned one-handed,
lopped its tips like a butcher topping bone –
some floated down that had the twigs to float
others dropped like sailors leaping overboard
knowing their ship to list beyond recall.

Higher he went and higher, stepping up
the branches like a ladder, till at the top
he ventured out like a tawny buzzard
perched on a bough too small
that bends beneath its weight.

He never looked concerned or faltered
but walked the boughs as a tight-rope walker
and yet not like, for where the walker likes
to keep us tensed up with his daring,
the feller made it seem he stood on ground

Down he came by stages with the tree –
soon its crown was gone, its rotted heart
uncovered – nothing left but the massive trunk
with sawn off stumps of arms. Using a looped rope
the feller legged his way as from a steeple.

They sawed the base and fixed a wedge
cut a sink and kept a hinge for the tree to sever –
the chain quivered, took the strain – the tractor
eased forward – the trunk rose, up-righted,

                                         then fell
exposing the wall, the power lines and the cottage

The tree lay like a fallen statue
a colossus of wood with a core of peat,
the rings to count were fused together.
And now there was nothing to see but sky
and a single trunk where before had been two.

*The following poems are the result of BSE and TB
(tuberculosis). Anyone interested at all in the country
must be aware of the suffering to farmers when their stock
has to be slaughtered before their time. BSE was horrific
because of its threat to humans, but it is TB that lingers
on. Often it is a precious heifer that is taken from a herd
bred up over the years and in that sense, irreplaceable,
although the compensation is theoretically fair. TB is a
menace to farmers on all counts, it prohibits animal
movement, prevents sales, stops the letting of land where
cattle reactors have grazed. The tests are frequent and
time consuming, and cattle farmers dread them...*

Cattle

I saw you each day in the fields,
smelled your green munching breath
watched your tongues tearing
or heads raised, fine eyes glowing
out of mist's grey.

The slope fell away –
hills stumbled undulating to nothingness
a final line, then sky. A sombre knowledge
of betrayal grew as the sun came through

its rays catching your backs
turned them gold –

then as suddenly – black.

Loading

One by one they enter the yard
solemn bullocks, curious, ambling
towards the hay-rack, the mineral-
block, the shelter of the lean-to.
The wind lifts the sheet
of corrugated iron that slaps down
shattering silence.

The animals stand unmoved,
tails hunched to rain that settles
like dew on their tight-curled coats.
I brush my hand along, make a dark
patch that spreads like blood
that stains the cement beneath
hung carcasses.

One comes forward, sniffs my hand,
recoils, its big ears seem to look,

its large eyes glow out of mist's dark.
Together we wait, listen to moist
noises in a mute background,
the shift, the stamp, the dull thump
of head against another's rump.

A truck rattles with the known
shiver of wood and metal, the change
of tone as it enters the yard, draws up,
lowers the ramp. One by one
the bullocks mount, ride and plunge,
hit the sides. Slatted gates slam
on the slippery conveyor.

*The longed for summer can arrive in April only to absent
itself in May, but is a severe disappointment if it has not
come by June because by the end of June the days start to
shorten again, hay is beginning to go to seed and needs
cutting in July to be at its best. Back in the '60s, '70s
'80s small oblong hay-bales were made by a baler
sounding its own unique thumping rhythm; it is now
more often done with a Round or Big Baler and carried
by a tractor with a front-end loader. In 2004 one person
can take haymaking on alone, usually a man because of
the sheer weight of handling machinery to connect and*

disconnect, even with the help of the hydraulic lift. But it does save the back-breaking carrying and throwing up of small bales and has added the 'elevator' to a growing collection of redundant hay-making machinery of which the 'spider-wheel' or 'acrobat' was by far the most beautiful – a strange reminder of Van Gogh's paintings...

Hay

7 a.m.

out of the silence comes the rumble
of vehicles gathering force –
equipped

markets empty, high pressure is forecast

clouds roll over the heavy line of hill.
I smell it now, the scent of mown grass
indescribable, inimitable, sweet as babies' hair

air is thick with it
invasive as perfume
sprayed on a wrist
hay's trail leads up the stony track to the barn
purple vetch clings to tousled banks

hay wraps wire
stubble spikes my ankles as if resenting
its beheading, the toppled acres
of shivering grass

The barn interior seduces, cools
round bales pile tier on tier –
a disorderly theatre peopled by giants

these bales take charge – one falling could kill

dwarfed, I touch a shining curve
hard and unyielding, ignominiously bound
restricted from offering even in winter
before a knife slashes string

Outside a tractor's beat churns

the mower's spinning blade
cuts a path with grim precision
across a field misty with seed-heads –
swathes fall sleek as a girl's hair
sensuous even in death.

During the '80s and early '90s I was involved in the theatre as a playwright and used to think it a pity we always seemed to be in rehearsal during the only hot months of the year. There was usually another person to work on the farm — at one time a 'share-farmer'. But labour costs were rising. Young farmers and workers — often farmers' children unable to buy houses because of soaring prices, the steep rise of the tourist industry, and the popularity of the area for second homes — were forced into the towns. Short-sighted governments after the war, even up until the mid-'60s, could have bought up small decaying farm cottages at very low prices, done them up, and used them as a form of Council House to enable local people to stay on the land if they wished.

My favourite and particularly beautiful stretch of Ford's land lies along the valley of the Hayne Brook. Jim, our original stockman, told us it was named the Frogs' Parlour; it is semi-natural bog woodland, in the past turned over by tinners and as a result giving a different soil to the usual wet valley. Trees fall and re-seed or simply grow up out of the old roots...

Summer's passion

Down by the stream I smell the moist scent
                                          of grass
ripped by cattle grazing, feel the sun on bare arms,
a warmth that enfolds like the eyes of a lover

Days of summer are like balm on winter living
the softness of sphagnum moss under alder,
the sensual smell of resin oozing from pine

A purple cloud rises, absorbs the sky
                                          casting shadow –
thunder mumbles, repeats, fades into nothing

Inside the wood insects flicker,
zig-zag in clouds against black gaps
barring the way to a stream's bed of silted sand

A batter of rain strikes on leaves
beats them on to the water's pock-marked surface –
I stick out my tongue like a child to feel rain's kiss

hear its hiss as it sweeps through trees
rushes on in ecstasy: sodden ground glistens

matted grass droops exhausted by the onslaught

I breathe in the humid smell of undergrowth
walk out on to open ground steaming under sun

Invader

This wood is uncharted, a narrow strip of green
marked on the map. Its twisted trees contort –
shadow carefully lays black trunks
into its depths, its bog

I tread carefully, know where it permits
and where I am trespassing
Flag-iris' laze on bog's surface
flower yellow as the gold sieved by tinners

Ancient, mined out, commercially worthless –
home of alder, young and upright, old and leaning,
                                        or fallen to rot
Ash and hazel form its rim preferring the stony
                                        ground
the thrown up dross
A monstrous tree lies part buried part grasping at air

Grey days and still.

Here a cat carried her kitten to raise under a rock

Bog sucks each boot
water oozes, sinks suspiciously –
green laces over sodden black soil –

ferns unfurl from brittle sheaves
in islands – stepping stones

Pausing, I hear tiny unrecorded noises
like a sucking at earth's breast –
I'm the stranger here

the invader.

Crossing the Frogs' Parlour

Chestnut, gold, black backs
lurch between lichened trunks –
water falls in a pool of kingcups,
purslane stars the banks, birds-eye
rings rocks – bluer than sky,
than sea, than stained glass.

The casual cattle plough
the water of a clean stream
splayed over a sand bed,
break branches from rotten alder
to float like severed limbs.
Hooves echo on a slab of clapper
the stream has altered course
forgotten the bridge left
muddied-up, grown over
revealed only by a sounding.

One by one, emerging
from the narrow way,
the herd fan across a yellow meadow
wreathed in May.

The path lies ravished
each print cups water
the soup thick body of stream
slithers through a dam of sticks.

*Mining, primarily for tin but also copper, was a part of
the moor up until 1930 when the last mine closed. In
mediaeval times the moor, often described as an empty
wilderness, was heavily populated owing to both mining*

*and the wool trade. Gold, found alongside tin, still
remains but is now generally in places where permission
would not be granted to mine it out (for instance the
Crediton Trench) Even so, the keen panner can find small
deposits in some of the moor streams and until recently
when the dual carriageway intervened, could pan the
Dart...*

Gold

I only valued you when you had gone,
slipped from the pan of life like gold
gone over the lip, swilled too fast –
a glinting colour poured back with all the rest

I remember that day last summer, early
– before the tourists blossomed
in primary colours on shining bikes –
how the two of us panned along the river

how I got only stones and lumps of tin
while your pan flashed the unmistakable yellow.
By night we'd eight flakes picked
and stored in phials: you were immeasurably happy

no money could have bought it off you.
You fused it into a thin sheet beaten,
said it would make me a pendant.
Now I sit fingering the gold chain

bought to suspend it, and think of your
meticulous spirit planning
an alchemy to forge for me
the failing glint of fast receding stars

The most recent poems are of indecision. Both of us are
well past the age when most farmers retire, but cannot
quite bring ourselves to leave the land. As regards the
farm, we have cut back our stock to a small bunch of cows
and calves and a further bunch of young stock – heifers
and steers. The land we let as far as possible, but with
the pressure of cattle disease, either to our own or our
neighbours' herds, it is an uncertain business. We let the
mowing grass and make hay to sell and for ourselves.
How much longer we can continue even in this pattern I
don't know; at the moment the income gained from
farming is negligible, and to keep going many farmers
practice some other form of business as well...

I thought of selling our house...

then thought again of the pink sky
through leaded windows –
the frosty grey of fields waiting for sun –
the untidy trees like a hastily dressed woman
nothing arranged, nothing final.

The massive beech with branches
curved down stands naked
waiting for spring to deck it out
in lime green leaves, pale and perfect,
turning its boughs black.

The cat is on me, purring –
the telephone sits mute, coiled, a snake
ready to strike cancelling the illusion
of isolation. My mother's chest of drawers
regards me as it did her – the stool
has strayed from the dressing-table,
the mirror above too high to see a face.
These inanimate things must move with me,
find a new position, help me settle.

For bit by bit I'm becoming redundant,

an out-dated wardrobe, a receptacle waiting
to be opened or shut, at most an audience
for the changing moods of sky –
the oddity of trees –
the stranglehold of early morning frost.
I lie listening to the persistent coo of doves
waiting for sun to unwrap
rigid blades of grass on a north face.

The owls called all night...

the doves have taken over,
fluttering, dislodging lichen off the roof.
People came to see this place
with a view to buying –
a man and a woman.

They had a map, walked round.
I told them all the best places.
My heart came to my mouth
bled at the thought.
I was afraid.

When I saw them there
as though it was theirs

it suddenly became mine –
like your child that takes
another's hand, walks away.

There was the money to consider,
everyone said – and the climate,
no sun for three hundred days in the year.

I walked in the fields that evening,
saw a kite's paper tail strewn
across the sky after the sun had set
over the whale's back of black hill
that sees it down.

The fields after hay,
the calving in snow –
ice on the roads, the stiff
bodies of lambs.
I thought of the work,
the mud and the rain,
the monotony of seasons
that re-occur like a clock.

By this I am held
intangibly as moon

trapped by the earth
drags at the tides.

Wild Cherry

The wild cherry is out.
It tangles branches
with another
dangles long cascades of lace.
The moor is still bare and brown
but most of the trees
are tinted green.
Narcissi jitter: there is always wind.

This place is eternally cold,
cold but exquisite like
someone too perfect to leave –
cold as the waters of Lethe and as dark.

In winter I grope my way round like a mole,
longing for light from the transient summer
that comes and goes. I huddle against
the opened stove, let warmth creep up my back.
This is a house that eats life –
old and seductive.

Demanding
I have I lived here too long –
am sucked dry. Yet to leave
is like abandoning an infant
in a church porch.
Change will come.
Conversion.
Voices will shout across clear cold air.

The swallows will soon cease
to search for a hole in the barn window,
knock against glass. The opened half
of the stable door has gone. No barn owl
glides ghostly-white across the pond field at dusk.
The bats are gone from the lofts –
jackdaws cling to corrugated iron
eyeing new tiles.

No doves bathe in the leat.

Clearing the Office

I helped you clear the office,
carried bursting cardboard boxes

photograph albums, papers,
staggered under loads of files,
piled them on the kitchen table
till it mounted up and spread
awkwardly as ill-planned housing
Once the room was cleared
I read relief all over your face.
The straw mat lay rotted
on the lawn: tables nudged
under loads of junk: electric wires,
extensions, lumps of tin
muddled with semi-precious stones

The room waited for plaster
like a body in an undertakers' parlour –
dirty-white panelled walls
with spider-darkened corners
showed damp along the skirting –
a radiator pulled from the wall
lay under a shelf lodged lopsided

The builder came, built a sill
of home grown oak: the room
gained a fine face, a new skirting,
a floor shining with the sheen

of years of tread, a sea-grass carpet
laid beneath a cow's skin,
a coat of ice-white silk finish

Bit by bit you shifted back the boxes
made it look just as it was before.

*And finally as I began with my mother I feel this poem is
due to her because it was she who not only instilled me
with a love of the country, farming and wildlife but also
my own children...*

A symbol for my mother

My mother's grave is in the churchyard
her granite headstone seldom tended
rises out of new grass.
Daisies grow round it,
celandines and birdseye –
she would have liked that,
she lived that sort of life
waiting for spring, bent over
flower pots, filling watering cans.
The green house was her friend,

tomatoes turned slowly from green
to red – begonias stiffened – geraniums stank.

When she died the greenhouse dried.
Boys threw stones at the glass –
pigeons and crows entered, pecked
the tomatoes' flesh, spilt their seeds.
The lawn grew lank.

I didn't think about it at the time,
how much it was a symbol for my mother,
conquering life, creating order, breeding
out of a 'dead land'. When arthritis
finally imprisoned her in bed
she turned her face from her garden
looked at vases of cut flowers –
asked no more of living.

It is indisputable that the changes since 1959 have been immense. To start with the two of us are on our own, I have become the stock person and Christopher does just about everything else. We use contractors and are helped by our neighbour when in difficulties. We rent our land as much as possible except for what we need for our own small herd, and make hay to sell and for ourselves. Also sell wood from our own timber. We just about tick over for farm income – I make an uncertain amount from writing.

There are far more people living here now who don't farm and commute to work, and many farmers have been forced out by a reduced income in part owing to cattle diseases, and consequently have been tempted to sell at the high prices this area now commands – not for the land but for the houses. Most barns have been converted and almost all the workers' cottages bought up or used for holiday lets. Bed and breakfast in the main farm house is no longer the custom. In our village there remains only the church, a semi-modern village hall, and the pub which has been vastly enlarged to cater for summer coach tours. The rector lives in an adjoining parish; the nearest shop is 6 miles away and everyone goes everywhere by car. The school bus still remains to ferry children over long distances.

No longer are bullocks driven along the road to

market as they still were in '59, but – and this is a consequence of change that is excellent – the new car mobility for this area has brought with it the advantage of schools improved beyond recognition, enabling children from all families to go to University or follow careers of their choice. A blossoming of talent in music, dance and drama has ensued, nurtured by South Dartmoor Community College and MED community theatre based on the moor.

Often it is the farmers who are criticised but over the years they have endeavoured to do what has been asked of them by Government, from the modernisation of buildings, the planting of quantities of softwoods, the removal of 'weeds', to the complete present reversal. No longer is food production the prime aim but the National Park Authority's policy of conservation – the wildlife, the keeping of the ancient, and the appearance of the environment. At one point in the late '60s an agricultural Advisor from the Midland Bank (now HSBC) suggested we remove the old buildings at Easdon and build a covered yard to alleviate our overdraft – at another in the late '70s the National Park Authority themselves told us Easdon Bottoms were of 'no ecological value'. Change has come, and fortunately we were not convinced enough to act on either pronouncement.

Farming now is seldom done by teams of workers as depicted in photos and records of the past, and the help farmers most often demand of each other is in the complicated struggle to fill in forms – a seemingly unending and time consuming task. Today it is not easy to run a farm without a computer – in fact it is not easy to run a farm at all now that a licence is needed to even shift healthy stock from one adjacent farm to another.

For myself, I imagine my love/hate relationship with farming has become transparent. It is the land set in the moor and created by farmers out of rock and scrub over hundreds of years that I have grown to care for and love – and the animals that perpetuate it by grazing.